SPIRITUAL ENERGY HEALING:

REIKI, KUNDALINI, MINDFULNESS

3-in-1 Bundle

THE ULTIMATE SET OF GUIDED MEDITATIONS FOR STRESS AND ANXIETY RELIEF, CHAKRAS AND THIRD EYE OPENING

By Anne Brennan

PUBLISHED BY SOLARIUS PRESS

CONTACT@SOLARIUSPRESS.COM

VISIT WWW.MEDITATIONCOLLECTION.COM

TABLE OF CONTENTS

SPIRITUAL ENERGY HEALING

The ultimate introduction and guided Reiki meditation
to reduce stress, increase energy and open your chakras

ANNE BRENNAN

INTRODUCTION

In a world of unlimited material distractions and technological disruptions, it's incredibly easy to lose your inner sense of self. Both your internal and external perceptions of the world are torn in many different directions every day, polluting your spirit with unessential worries and frustrations. I wrote this book to suggest a few time proven methods to let go of those worries and frustrations. You will become more resilient, better focused, and better acquainted with your intuition. It takes daily concentration to identify the universe's unseen energies. I am convinced that it is a worthwhile investment of your time to learn to direct the flow of those energies for your benefit.

As I'm sure you know, energy healing is a powerful tool that anyone can learn to harness if they have the commitment and dedication to do so. It is not the most straight forward practice, however, which is why this book is designed to help you get started as effectively as possible. The following chapters will walk you through preparations for effective meditation and provide you with a set of guided meditations centered on the Japanese practice of **Reiki**. These meditations are most effective if practiced daily. They will transport your astral body to a personalized plane of serenity.

I know that there are many books out there, promising you the benefits of spiritual energy healing. So I thank you from the bottom of my heart for choosing my book.

Please, enjoy!

With much love,
Anne Brennan

CHAPTER 1

INTRODUCTION TO REIKI

Reiki is considered a healing art based in Japan. Reiki comes from the word *rei* meaning "*universal life*" and *ki* which translates to "*energy*." Reiki is not tied to any specific religion or religious practices nor does it push a specific belief system. Reiki is an effective and subtle form of energy work that uses guided life force energy.

This life energy flows through everything. Reiki practitioners understand that everyone needs to connect to their own healing energy and strengthen it to help themselves and others. Most people believe that a person's energy needs to flow freely. This will be effective whenever a person's mind and body are in a positive state of health; but when their energy is weak or blocked, it can lead to physical and emotional imbalances.

Reiki therapy involves touch and is meant to assist the body to heal itself from common ailments that it is dealing with. Reiki practitioners are able to tap into the natural energy of the body in order to remove any blockage and to redirect the flow of misdirected or stagnant energy. This can help to promote the health and wellness inside the individual.

Reiki is primarily focused on the chakras, or the energy centers, of the body. These energy centers allow the practitioner to stimulate the healing abilities that are found naturally inside of the body. Through straightening, healing, and clearing the flow of energy through the body, it is possible to resolve many of the common ailments that are going on inside of the body, including emotional, mental, and physical problems.

When you do not take care of your energy imbalances, it is going to cause some physical ailments inside of the body. In fact, many of the diseases and illnesses that go on inside the body are due to these energy imbalances. Reiki is able to come in and solve some of these problems, opening up those energy centers so that you feel much better.

Reiki is also known as a form of mental therapy because it has the ability to impact your psychological conditions, like depression and anxiety, in a positive manner. In fact, those who have practiced Reiki often feel a better sense of well-being and improved self-confidence when they are done.

Reiki can work well for so many people because it is gentle and non-invasive, which is completely different compared to the other forms of alternative healing Rather than focusing all that energy on the symptoms of a condition, Reiki treats the whole person, helping to send healing energy in the direction that it is needed the most.

REIKI AND CHAKRAS

Everywhere around us, there is an energy that is constantly changing. Our bodies soak up this energy like a sponge and it is absorbed through your chakras.

Awareness to the chakras in the human body has been around since before the new age and they play a vital role in yoga. In Sanskrit, the word chakra literally means "*wheel of light*" and that is how chakras should be looked at – as a gift, especially to those that can see them. When someone can see them, they appear as spinning colored light wheels. Each chakra appears as a different color on the rainbow spectrum.

Each chakra is aligned along the spinal column and they form the backbone that connects the body, mind, and spirit. This network includes several smaller energy centers throughout the body and typically corresponds with acupuncture points.

During a Reiki session, the hands will be placed on the major chakras as well as the secondary chakras, which are typically dysfunctional and discolored or even closed off completely because of problems with one's mind, spirit, or body. It is important to keep these gateways open because if there is a disruption in the energy flow, then one may lead to illness.

As I mentioned earlier, Reiki treatments are supposed to help clear out energy blockages in the chakras while restoring the flow of one's life force energy. Energy flows in and out of one's aura through the chakras. This aura is a light that envelopes every person. The aura is composed of seven layers, each one dealing with the various aspects of our being. The major chakras create a cone around the core of the spine throughout every layer of our aura.

In one's physical body, each major chakra corresponds with an endocrine gland that helps to control the hormonal balance and a major nerve plexus.

At the base of the spine, there is the *root chakra*; between the genitals and naval is the *sacral chakra*; above that is the *solar plexus chakra*; in the middle of the chest is *the heart chakra*; in the middle of the neck is *the throat chakra*; below the brow is *the third eye chakra*; and at the top of the head is *the crown chakra*.

THE THIRD EYE AND REIKI

As I mentioned earlier, your third eye chakra is located between your eyes. It deals with intelligence and psychic power.

As you perhaps know from biology, *hormones* are responsible for how the body functions. Hormones are tied to many aspects of your body including the physical, emotional, and mental aspects. Modern day Reiki practitioners relate chakras to the *endocrine system*.

For your physical health, the third eye governs the pineal gland along with your eyes, ears, nose, and the skeletal system. It is tied to the senses of sight and hearing as well as one's ability to form their own opinions about the world around them and how they are going to live.

Your third eye secretes a hormone known as *melatonin* which regulates your sleep cycle and growth and also slows down the aging process while maintaining a stable mind. This gland is sensitive to light which makes most people believe that the eyes are stimulated from the pineal gland when melatonin is released. Many scientists think that the electromagnetic field of the earth is also responsible for stimulating this gland.

Your pineal gland governs your eyes and how you see the world around you, as well as any psychic and intuitive abilities you may have.

The third eye chakra plays a vital role in determining how alert you will be, as well as help with how clearly you see things and how optimistic you are while you visualize the outcomes you want. This chakra will create a reality for you that can become real based on your perception. Whenever this chakra is balanced, you will have the ability to visualize better and your memory will become sharper. You should trust yourself that you can be able to rely on your intuitions. You will also be able to help someone without them requesting for your help.

An imbalanced third eye chakra causes problems in understanding reality or creating our own. You may find that you are relying too much on luck and blaming someone when a bad situation happens. Your headache will cause trouble on you which will also lead to having a constant feeling of anxiousness. You may find that you want to dominate or control others. If you experience these things, then your third eye is most likely blocked.

CHAPTER 2

<hr>

THE PRACTICAL GUIDE TO REIKI MEDITATIONS

To prepare your mind, you'll want to speak the Reiki Ideals. Say the words from your heart and mind, as well as your lips. As you are repeating the Reiki Ideals, put your hands, palms together, in front of your heart chakra as illustrated on the picture below.

Before you begin, invite your inner spirit to participate in this self-healing process. You will be the healer and the healed as you practice Reiki's self-healing discipline.

Think of this as a *Reiki prayer*. It should be done with a reverent and open heart. This is not a time to be skeptical or doubtful, but rather a time of knowing that you are about to be introduced to your helper and comforter, your strength and guide. Breathe deeply; focus on slowly inhaling through your nose and then just as slowly exhaling through your mouth. When you have released all the air from your lungs, let your breath drift off then hold it for about five to six seconds longer before slowly releasing the remaining air from your passage ways.

Invite Reiki to guide your energy throughout every cell of your body, touching the areas that require healing. Continue to feel the relaxing rhythm of your heart as Reiki responds to your gentle requests for calmness, peace, and healing.

To be completely prepared for your session, do this first Reiki pose each evening for three or four days before your full session to come. This will help to open your chakras and encourage your mind to freely and fearlessly seek Reiki before your first session and be fully prepared to release what binds you.

Only ask and invite during these first few evenings, staying calm and relaxed, prayerfully seeking Reiki's wisdom and healing power for your first full session. Remember to thank Reiki for all that you are about to experience. Make sure you get plenty of rest and drink lots of water to wash away the negatives.

REIKI SYMBOLS

Reiki has its own three sets of symbols representing its own arena or its own category of assumptions.

The first group of symbols is called *Tattwa*. There are five different symbols in this group, each representing a different element of the universe. I.e. earth, air, water, fire, spirit. They reign over the realm of energy in the brain. This group of symbols may also affect other areas such as realities that are not physical like dreams.

The next symbol group is *physical items* such as Rosaries. They have the ability to be charged with the power of a ritual or connection with holy places to cause an effect.

The final group of symbols are less straightforward. These are *devices or triggers* like the Reiki symbols learned earlier, that enable the use of Reiki energy. These symbols offer a pathway to connection with energy that is independent.

The symbols are not the exclusive means of accessing Reiki energy. They will make your Reiki experience much more gratifying or satisfying. If you don't know the exact meaning of any given symbol you may still use it; you will gain wisdom with time and practice.

The Master Symbol of Reiki is called *'DAI KO MYO'*. It holds the greatest power. It is used for a much deeper, spiritual healing. It enhances one's intuition and can change your life dramatically. The Master Reiki symbol is made of three kanji's (characters). One means *great* or *greatly*. The second means *light* in noun form or *smooth* as an adjective. This kanji may also mean *completely*. The final kanji is an adjective or a verb. It may mean *evident* or *see, understand*. Put together, the three kanji's mean *great bright light*.

Remember, you may use all or only selected symbols, they are not a necessary ingredient in Reiki. They do bring enhancement to the energy flow. You may, of course, choose to use none.

Like earlier mentioned symbols, these can be activated in numerous ways. You might draw or visualize a symbol or you may chant. You might form the shape in your mouth with the tip of your tongue. How you activate is up to you.

PREPARE YOUR CHAKRAS

Prior to using Reiki meditation on yourself, you are going to want to ensure that your chakras are open and ready for the experience as well. The following technique will also work well with the Kundalini meditation discussed in a separate book in my series *'Spiritual Energy Healing: Kundalini'*. While you are welcome to work through the entire process each time, you may instead simply want to focus on the parts that deal with the chakras that are bothering you the most.

For starters, you will work on the *root chakra* which you can start doing by simply focusing on the color red. When you start focusing on the color the odds are pretty good that it is a dull, dark red as opposed to a strong, vibrant red which should be your ultimate goal. Throughout your time working with this chakra you are going to want to focus on the color until it is bright and pulsating.

After you have opened up your root chakra, you will be ready to move on to the *sacral chakra* which is associated with the color orange which you will want to focus on making shine as brightly as possible. In fact, each chakra has its own color and you will want to focus on it as you work to make that particular chakra shine. You will want to make your way up the body until you reach *the crown chakra*. Once you have done so you can expect all of your chakras to be fully opened which means you are ready to move forward with Reiki meditation.

It is important to understand that this method is not something that you are going to see results with overnight. I'd like to warn you that depending on how tarnished your chakras are it could take literally *weeks* of diligent effort to get them shining brightly. Thus, if this is your first time with this practice or you simply haven't done it in a while then it is important to leave yourself enough time to do it properly without feeling rushed.

GASSHO MEDITATION

Another technique that you are able to use as part of Reiki meditations is known as *Gassho Meditation (Gassho means "two hands coming together")*. This method is going to take about five to fifteen minutes where you will focus all of your attention just on Reiki. It is beneficial to do this for each day. I'm aware of some programs that recommend doing it for at least 21-days to see how you like it. I think it's a good suggestion.

The steps to Gassho meditation are pretty simple. You do not need to do a ton of things other than concentrate on the Reiki healing powers, do some deep breathing, and sit in the right position. The steps that you need for Gassho Meditation include:

• *Take your hands and hold them in a prayer position. This is traditionally leaving the hands, with palms together, touching and the fingers touching as well. Make sure that these prayer hands are right at the heart.*

• *When the hands are done, close your eyes.*

• *Start to breathe in the Reiki energy through your nose, taking in a nice deep breath rather than the fast and uneven breaths that you have been doing before.*

• *Once you are ready, it is time to exhale that breath through your whole body. This would include the physical body, the etheric body, the mental body, and the spiritual body.*

You would just keep on with the deep breathing for as long as you needed, concentrating on the Reiki healing power as you go. Of course, there are a few different variations that you can try with this. Some people like to add these in because they allow them something to concentrate on or because they think that it adds some more power.

You can choose to write down a goal and then ask that some sort of clarification comes to you throughout your session. You can add in some music, as long as it is soft and inspiring in some manner or even chants a mantra. If you are dealing with a big problem in your life, you could ask for some help and guidance to get through that problem. Some people decide to draw the power symbol, the mental or emotional symbol, or the distance symbol over their body when they first get started. You are able to choose the variation that works the best for you or you can stick with the steps that are listed above to help you.

Before we get to our guided Reiki meditations, I would like to share with you a short daily Reiki Meditation, which you may use whenever you feel it's the right moment. It doesn't require a lot of time and with regular practice it can be a very good solution to reduce stress, increase energy and work on opening your chakras.

10 Minute Reiki Meditation

Lay or sit down comfortably on a mat. Keep your back straight. Stay relaxed, composed, and calm. Breathe deeply.

Imagine that you are inhaling the goodness and happiness that you want. Now exhale all the negative emotions like anxiety, fear, and depression. Imagine them leaving your body. Do this a few times and think about how in tune your mind and body are.

Just relax.

There are seven different chakras in the body. They go from the bottom of your spine to the top of your head. These are energy centers for the body. Put your hand in front of each chakra and hold it for a few minutes. This all depends on what your body needs. If your body asks for it to stay longer, leave it there. Move it if the body has enough. Feeling with the hands is the best way to listen and connect to your body. As you tune in with your hands, imagine the universe's life force is entering your body through the hands.

Your chakras are the passageway. Feel your body vibrate with the energy flow. Go into deep relaxation and rejuvenation.

Put your palms together at the top of your head. Hold your hands there and listen to your body. Pay attention. Continue to do this and breathe slowly and deeply. Remove all the negative and bring all the positives into you. Relax.

Put your hands on your forehead. Now move them to the back of your head. Move down to the throat and put on hand on the throat and the other at the back of the neck. Hold this for a time and relax.

Continue down and put your hands on the back of your shoulders. Your fingers should be facing downward. Your touch needs to be gentle. Hold your hands still until the body is ready for it to be moved.

Put your hands on your chest covering your heart. Remember to hold until the body tells you to move.

Move on to the rib area, then the stomach and lower abdomen. Keeping your touch gentle and moving when the body is ready.

When you are done with the head and torso, move to the hips and put your hands on both your hips. Moving only when the body tells you to. Feel the energy flowing through the body. Enjoy the sensations.

Move on to your knees and feet. For your feet, place the hands either on bottom or top whichever is more comfortable. Move your hands when your body is ready. Enjoy the experience.

Finally, place your hands in the prayer position and put them in front of your chest. Sit with the spine straight and the body taut. Breathe normally. Feel the energy coursing through your body.

Continue this for another three to five minutes or as long as you feel the need.
This process is done when you feel energized and ignited.

CHAPTER 3

PREPARATION AND

LOGISTICS

Now, the time has come to prepare yourself for our Reiki guided meditations. First of all, you will need to make yourself physically comfortable in a safe space in which you can unwind and open yourself to cosmic energies.

Ready your environment. Declutter your surroundings. Create a space that will not distract you from navigating your own spiritual journey. Perhaps light a scented candle or a stick of incense. A soothing aroma may help guide your senses to a more pleasurable frame of mind. A sweet wave of lavender or vanilla may provide you with a calmness otherwise unfounded in your chosen space of meditation. The earthy tones of sandalwood or lemongrass may help lull you into a trance, a state of mind susceptible to spiritual guidance. You may prefer nectarous scents like a mandarin orange or red apple. Let the candle's flame flicker. Let the incense stick pour its smoke.

Perhaps, brew yourself a cup of herbal tea. Establish a connection with nature by ingesting a steeped herb, flower, or root. Allow the sweet, earthy liquid to clear your nasal passages. Unencumbered breathing is integral to meditation. A steaming cup of tea will warm your insides and loosen your muscles by relieving them of unwanted stress. It will help your body sink into your meditation. Let the tea replenish your body with essential antioxidants and vitamins. Tune your body with this natural remedy.

Are you wearing comfortable clothing? It is crucial that what you are wearing does not inhibit your ability to breathe. Loose fitting clothing or breathable fabrics are recommended. Is the temperature of your space to your liking? Will a lack or excess of warmth or cold break your concentration? Adjust your setting. Create a space that's right for you.

Choose a spot to sit or lie down. Do not engage in meditation while engaged in other activities like walking or driving. Your body must be stationary, you must be open and ready to receive spiritual guidance. Allow yourself to concentrate on the journey ahead.

Perhaps you have a favorite chair in which to sit on. A bed, a couch, or a cushioned mat on the floor are also acceptable places to situate yourself for a session of meditation. Fluff your pillows or cushions. Ready your favorite fuzzy blanket. Maybe employ a face mask to black out your surroundings. Allow your body to sink into whatever space you choose.

Distance yourself from polluting noise. It is unideal to allow in loud engines on the road, trains chugging past, loud voices outside your window, rattling footsteps, dogs barking, cats hissing, dump trucks clunking along, or the ringing of a phone. Silence your phone and shut down your computer. Separate yourself from the noise. Use headphones or a loud enough speaker set to listen to the meditations. Submerge yourself in the journey, and eliminate any possible distractions. All five senses must be wholly committed to the journey in order to achieve ultimate relaxation.

CHAPTER 4

GUIDED REIKI MEDITATIONS

BEFORE WE BEGIN

In this chapter I would like to share with you my Reiki guided meditations which aim to balance your inner energy. The ultimate goal is to help you feel grounded and content.

First, I will I guide you into a *deep state of relaxation*. Then we will continue with the main *Reiki meditation*.

The effects of Reiki healing are best received when sitting in an upright position. If you are lying down, please sit up. Do not cross your legs. Open your palms to the sky, rest them on the top of your knees. Comfortability is still central to these meditations.

You must be completely open to accepting this process. Take a moment to get in touch with the Supreme Being in which you believe. Let their positive force into your space. Invoke their power.

Now, take a moment to focus intently on the points in your body that are experiencing pain. Attempt to see these areas with your eyes closed. Each of the following Reiki meditation steps will focus on a different chakra starting from the **root chakra**, *Muladhara*, and ending with **the crown chakra**, *sahaswara*.

Now, take a breath in. Exhale the air and follow the meditation guide.

THE PATH TO RELAXATION

Close your eyes. Nothing else exists except this moment. Be here and now. Release your worries, let go of that weight. Close your eyes and embrace the blackness behind your lids. Breathe steady, breathe with purpose. Feel the life you breathe within yourself. Give thanks to your lungs for that breath.

Nothing else exists except this moment. The hours before this moment and the hours after this moment are not relevant to the journey ahead. Time is a construct, release yourself from its hold. Become consoled by the fact that nothing matters except the here and the now. Stay within the present.

Focus on your spirit and the energy around and within you. Liberate yourself from the confines of your physical body.

To start, you must alleviate your body and its muscles of all tension it has stowed away. While lying or sitting, curl your toes and release. Point your feet and return. Rotate your ankles. Briefly and gently flex your calves, your thighs, your glutes, your abdomen, your chest, your back, your upper arms, and your lower arms. Clench your fists and release. Rotate your wrists, then lay your palms flat. Unclench your jaw. Rest your tongue in your mouth. Flex your face muscles. Lie still and take this moment to focus on every inch of your body. Identify where any tension, no matter how small, may still be present. Exercise any tense area to relieve it of pressure. Once that is finished, continue lying or sitting still. Concentrate on sinking into the surface on which you sit or lie.

Give thanks to that surface for its support. You are safe and secure exactly where you are.

Embrace the blackness behind your lids. Let go of your reservations and prepare to embark on this journey with a weightless frame of mind. Let go of your worries like the strings of balloons. Watch the wind carry them up into space out of your sight. Your hands are free, you are free. Feel the weight rise from your shoulders. You are liberated of your burdens.

Nothing else exists except this moment. It is you and your spirit here and now. Sink into the blackness behind your lids. It will safely carry you to a state free of concern, free of doubt, and free of worry. Embrace the blackness. You will only need the vision of your third eye to guide you through this spiritual quest.

Out from the blackness rises a welcoming wave of water. The wave grows taller with each surge. Feel it in the tips of your relaxed toes. It rises to your calves, your thighs, your belly, your chest, your throat, and your shoulders. Let it run down your arms and into the tips of your fingers. Finally, let the wave wash over your head. Let its waters cleanse your mind, wipe it blank of the day's mental and spiritual interferences.

The wave is providing you with the perfect preparation for spiritual meditation and physical relaxation. The wave granting you the equanimity you need. The waters of the wave will be absorbed into you. Be hydrated, be full of the tranquil swell. Your stress is subdued above the surface. Your worries are out of range, out of sight, and out of mind and body. A rush of calm envelops you. The outside world cannot penetrate the surface of this strong wave. All that exists is here and now.

Breathe steadily. Release your fears into air around, let the universe filter it elsewhere. Create a distance between yourself and your demons. They are banished from this time and space. They are expelled by the wave. A wave of water, a wave of power, and a wave of light. A net has been cast to trap those excreted foes. They will not bother you during your journey. You are no longer oppressed by these insecurities, by these bothersome troubles. They will not be tangled in your spirit. Malignancy is wiped away. You are safe and you are secure.

Embrace the blackness behind your closed lids. The negative weight has been released, your body has been cleansed and fortified. You may now ready your body for the gradual addition of positive heaviness. This heaviness is welcomed. This heaviness will allow for you to stay grounded in your meditation. You will not budge from your protected space and time of peace. The heaviness is free of pressure and pain. You are preparing yourself to cross over, to disconnect with the physical world. This journey is for you, this voyage is personal.

You may often feel tied down to the physical world by restraints in the form of trepidation, stress, and fear. Untie those restraints. Unbind yourself. Feel a blue calm slowly run through your body. The calm is a ribbon of indigo, plum, and sapphire, an extension of the mighty wave. These gentle colors lull your body to a deep state of relaxation. Let the ribbon caress your limbs. It slowly circles around your left leg, your hips, your right leg, your waist, your chest, your left arm, your right arm, and it stops at your neck. Its silk enchants your physical form. The soft, woven threads help you feel in total control over your astral body.

Embrace the blackness behind your closed lids. Right here, right now, there are no materials. Here, there is no excess, here, there is no shortage. Here, everything is exactly as it should and where it should be. The heaviness has set in, the heaviness is a close friend. You have rejected the negativity and are now completely open to take the proper steps towards achieving enlightenment, towards achieving harmony.

You define the terms of your journey. Pay close attention to the energies flowing around and within you. Do not resist these energies. Be careful and considerate towards the energies that you sense. They are here with your spirit as you are guided through this journey.

Reiki Meditation: Step One

The hands are suspended behind your lower back.

A circular motion is practiced to awaken the

energy of *kundalini*.

Feel the primal energy ignite at the base of your

spine.

Warmth spreads from your lower back to your

hips, and to your pelvis.

The hands are steady.

Feel the positive flow of energy circulating through

your back.

Through your hips.

Through your pelvis.

It soothes, it heals.

Aching joints are at rest.

Pained nerves are settled and relaxed.

The hands gradually move down to your upper
legs.
Feel the Reiki emanate throughout the muscle.
The hands travel further down your leg.
They hover slightly above your shin, and then
above your calf.
Focus on the muscles as they loosen.
Focus on the relief the hands bring.

The hands slowly travel back up your legs.
They stop right above your belly.

Reiki Meditation: Step Two

The healing hands are suspended over your pelvic
area.

Reiki is focused now on your sacral chakra,
svadhishana.

This is a creative energy force, a source of
sensuality.

This spot reaps the fruits of your labor, it filters
your pleasures.

Focus on this area to derive creativity from the
energy that flows.

Focus on this area to determine whether or not
your indulgences are unhealthy or excessive.

There is no judgment from the hands.

Be honest with yourself about your actions.

Reflect on the sources of your passions.

Feel gratitude for your physical and emotional expressions of self.

Think to yourself these phrases:

"I have love and respect for my body",

"I know how to read my desires",

"I have boundaries with myself and others", and

"My sexuality is sacred."

The hands travel up. They are now directly over your belly.

Reiki Meditation: Step Three

The hands linger over your belly.
Reiki is focused on your solar plexus chakra,
Manipura.
The hands make a slow, circular motion over your
chakra.
Allow the positive energy to flow and unblock any
hindrances in your digestive system.
Your belly is settling under the influence of the
hands.

Reflect on your personal goals.
Repeat words that will bring you success in your
endeavors as the hands stir the chakra's energy.
Reflect on your accomplishments.

Feel your chakra charge with potential energy to

carry you into your future.

It makes you steady in your personal will.

You know yourself better than anyone or anything

on this earth.

Own that power.

Feel its warmth in your belly.

Reiki Meditation: Step Four

The hands stop over the center of your chest.

Reiki is focused on the heart chakra, *Anahata*.

Your heart sustains your life.

It pumps blood throughout your capable body.

Feel its beating.

Feel as the energy intertwines with the magnificent

pulses of life within you.

Feel as Reiki opens you to love and be

compassionate.

These are powerful qualities of human life.

Affirm the positive aspects of your life.

While the hands are at work, reflect on your

accomplishments. Reflect on what you are grateful

for.

You are loved.

You show love to others.

You are a beckon of benevolence.

You act selflessly.

You see good in others.

You respect all forms of life.

You are never alone in this world.

Your heart connects you with all forms of life.

The hands move up to your neck. They stop there.

Reiki Meditation: Step Five

The hands curve over the throat, hovering slightly
above your skin.

Reiki is now focused on the throat chakra,
vishuddha.

This area grants you the ability to communicate
your thoughts out loud.

You have a voice to cry out blessings and love to
the world around you.

The hands rotate around your neck, they prepare
you to speak the truth.

Feel as your throat is coated with energy.

Your voice is valid.

Your voice is strong, you are articulate.

Let the energy soothe any soreness you may have
in your throat.

The hands fold out over each of your shoulders.

Feel the energy ebb and flow within you.

The hands make their way up to your head.
They stop at the center of your forehead.

Reiki Meditation: Step Six

The hands hover side by side over your forehead.
Reiki is focused on your third eye chakra, *ajna*.
This chakra radiates a silver stream of moonlight.
Open your mind to the unseen, to the unheard, and
to the unimagined.
Let the hands guide Reiki into the very core of
your mind, into the depths of your consciousness.
Tap into the astral plane in which your spirit exists.
See visions of your success and health with new-
found clarity.
Breathe in deeply.
Exhale deeply.
Focus on the area between your eyebrows.
Feel its sacred power.

The hands slowly move above your third eye chakra.

They are now above your head.

REIKI MEDITATION: STEP SEVEN

The hands are extended above your head.
Reiki is focused on the crown chakra, *sahaswara*.

The universe is infinitely expanding.
Reopen your mind to the possibilities that this
existence holds.
You hold the power to manifest whatever destiny
you so choose.
The hands are directing energy from a diverse
range of mediums from around the cosmos.
Absorb the energy of the unknown.
Acknowledge that there are things you have yet to
learn about yourself and those around you.
Feel excited by prospects of new-found life and
experience.

The hands rest here.

They do a final slow sweep of your body.

From the head to the forehead,

to the throat and shoulders,

down to the chest,

to the abdomen,

below the belly,

and back again to the base of your spine.

The Return

Now that the hands have completed their work,

take a moment to ruminate on your experience.

Focus on the current of energy flowing within you.

Keep in mind the areas that experience the most

difficulty in the process of unblocking the energies'

channels.

You are one of the infinite mediums through which

energies of the cosmos travel.

A mystical force runs through you.

From your root chakra, do you feel a primal power

pulsing?

Are you more grounded with your identity here on

earth?

You are secure here.

Take some time out of your day to reacquaint
yourself with the outside world.
Maintain a good relationship with nature.

From your sacral chakra, do you feel a swell of
creative energy?
Are you more open to accepting pleasure in your
life?
Enjoy the perks of being human.
Exercise your creativity and indulgence.

From your solar plexus chakra, do you feel a sense
of steadfast confidence?
Is your stomach well attuned?
You are a force of love and compassion.
You are capable of more than you yet know.

From your heart chakra, do you feel a radiant love
for all?

Do not waste your energy and resources on the act
of hate.
Take the time to understand what puzzles you.

From your throat chakra, do you feel the strength
to speak the truth?
You are blessed with the ability to speak.
Is there anything that you have been afraid or
reluctant to say?
It's important to communicate honestly in order to
live as authentically as you can.
Hone your personal truth with every word you
speak.

From your third eye chakra, do you feel wonderful
for the unknown?
Are you able to pick up on extrasensory activity
churning around you?
Focus on this area to receive subtle psychic
messages from the universe.

Acknowledge that there is more left for you to
learn.

From your crown chakra, do you feel a surge of
perception?
Has unwanted pressure and strain been excreted
from your mind?
Hopefully, you are more open to the vast stock of
wisdom held within the universe than ever before.

Take one last moment to focus on the energy
flowing through your muscles.
Until next time.

Namaste.

CONCLUSION

Thanks for making it through to the end of *Spiritual Energy Healing: Reiki*. I sincerely hope that reading this book was useful for you and I successfully guided you through refreshingly new or comfortably familiar ways to achieve inner peace. It's important to consistently acknowledge the energies working around you, how the energies affect you, and how you affect those energies. Be sure to constantly remind yourself that you are merely a small piece of a greater whole. Yet, just as the universe is infinitely expanding, so are you.

The next step is to make a ritual of your preferred meditation. Practicing every day helps guarantee the results you want to experience from meditation. Daily discipline will improve your concentration and ground your thoughts during your sacred times of personal rumination. Embed positivity within you. Don't sweat the small aspects of life.

You can also explore more resources that help you unlock deeper levels of harmony. To advance your spiritual journey, discover more about the practices and teachings of

Hinduism, Buddhism, and holistic Japanese techniques. Eastern cultures have an array of deeply spiritual history packed full of wisdom. Perhaps pay a visit to a Reiki healer near you. You may also enjoy yoga as a more physically involved form of meditation that utilizes similar meditative techniques found in my book.

With much love,
Anne Brennan

SPIRITUAL ENERGY HEALING

The ultimate introduction into Kundalini awakening and guided yoga meditation to open your chakras, heal your body and gain elightment

ANNE BRENNAN

CHAPTER 1

INTRODUCTION TO KUNDALINI

For more than 5,000 years, cultures all around the globe have sought to find and experience true enlightenment and divinity through spiritual and physical practices. Yoga, meditation, and other methods that are meant the bring unity between the spirit and the body are techniques that have been proven to awaken the *Kundalini*. Kundalini is an energy force that lies at the bottom of your spine; coiled like a snake that is waiting to rise up through your body and bring true spiritual awareness with your higher self. In fact, "Kundalini" comes from the Sanskrit word *"coiled up"* or *"coiling like a snake."* Early Eastern religions believed that every person has this divine energy that rests at the base of his or her spine.

Yoga was initially established in the Eastern world as a way to create a direct and intimate connection with the higher self and the divine. Those who practice awakening their Kundalini believe that everyone is capable of making this spiritual connection in order to develop a relationship and gain insight from the divine. Such individuals do not see a need for religious buffers such as priests or places of worship in order to receive information from the spiritual realm. All a person needs to do it connect with the divine-like spirit within themselves was to practice.

One of the most comforting factors of stirring your Kundalini is that it can be done anywhere at any time. You do not have to go to a fancy yoga studio, visit a guru, or pay a spirituality coach to help you. With enough studying, effort, and determination, anyone can awaken their Kundalini and experience enlightenment. While yoga is primarily a physical practice, Kundalini yoga is fixated on activating *chakras*, or energy centers, throughout your body to fully awaken your conscience. Kundalini is the ultimate means of awakening your higher self by reducing anxiety and the separation of the physical and spiritual selves, through learning the ability to connect with your inner self.

When you experience a Kundalini awakening, it will resolve all of the issues that come from a blocked psyche. It should be noted that most people can experience a small amount of energetic experience, but it is rare to have a full awakening. In the chapters to follow, I will provide you with the information to open each chakra that you may feel is blocked. As you move from the Mujadara to the Sahaswara, you will awaken your whole system.

Whether you experience a full awakening, or just the beginning stages, it is all the awakening of your Kundalini energy. The energy will move up from your spine in different shapes and forms. It should be noted that this awakening will not change depending on your country of origin, religion, or culture. The experience will be brought forth through spiritual traditions. In fact, when used, it is the natural evolution of your being to be altered into a higher level of consciousness.

KUNDALINI AWAKENING

In Kundalini, there are two widely known approaches to awakening your Kundalini. There is an *active* way as well as a *passive* way. If you choose the active approach, you will use a number of concentration techniques, physical exercise, as well as meditation, breath practice and visual guidance through a teacher.

If you decide to go with a passive approach, you will step away from actively trying to awaken your Kundalini. Through this process, the Kundalini will be awakened by an individual who has already experienced the awakening themselves. Through *Shaktipat* (Sanskrit word meaning *'transmission of spiritual energy'*), it is possible to raise the Kundalini temporarily. It will provide students with the needed sensation so they can use it as a base once they do try to awaken their Kundalini themselves.

In Hindu tradition, you can only experience a Kundalini awakening by purifying and strengthening your body. If a student wanted to open their Kundalini, they would have to follow this path with an open heart.

GUIDED AWAKENINGS

While no two Kundalini experiences are ever going to be exactly the same, each will often begin with a round of meditations. They are tuned specifically to maximize the potential from awakening the Kundalini from where it waits to rise throughout the body. This rising typically translates to a warming sensation that can be mild or intense as it moves up the spinal column. This rising of the Kundalini then coincides with an awakening of the chakras as its energy opens them all at once.

This warming feeling often suddenly gives way to extreme cold accompanied by shaking or shuddering. Some participants feel the need to rock back and forth, sometimes violently, others may experience multiple changes in temperature or see and/or hear things that they cannot explain. The goal is to keep up this ecstatic state until the Kundalini energy reaches all the way to the crown chakra.

After this occurs, the meditation moves on to lowering it back down in a measured state until it is just above the heart chakra. This is a crucial step as it is believed that lowering it back below the heart chakra too quickly is a surefire way to cause a number of negative side effects such as an increase in ego, wanton sexual desire and more.

With practice, the level of Kundalini energy in the body at all times will remain higher, naturally leading to a more permanent opening of the chakras along with an overall improved sense of awareness. This will naturally occur over time as the Kundalini energy is able to create new pathway s through your body through which its energy can then pass. This process can be painful at times as the nervous system has to learn to adapt through the new energy regularly flowing through it. Experts at the practice of Kundalini meditation warn that it is important to start off slowly as it can be draining to open yourself up to too much of the energy all at once.

CHAPTER 2

MUDRAS AND CHAKRAS

INTRODUCTION TO MUDRAS

Kundalini meditations rely on *mudras*. Mudras are hand positions that each have a purpose. Mudras help to stimulate nerves or activate glands. The mudras act as a way to talk and connect with our bodies in order to aid in clearing the mind. Practice positioning your hands into mudras and get to know what they are called. Learn what each mudra is meant to help with.

The posture for knowledge (Gyan Mudra) is one that you may have more familiarity with. This is when the thumb and index finer touch, leaving the other fingers straight. This posture helps with patience and commitment.

Another mudra you are probably already familiar with is the *prayer pose (Pranam Mudra)*, which is simply the hand in a prayer position in front of the heart center. Familiarize yourself with some of the more well-known mudras as Kundalini meditation uses many of them.

The abhayamudra is also known as *the gesture of fearlessness,* it represents peace, protection, the overcoming of fear and benevolence. It is made with the right arm bet and held at roughly shoulder height with the palm facing straight ahead with the fingers close and pointing upright with the left hand resting naturally on the left.

The bhumisparsa mudra is more commonly known as *the earth witness mudra* and is one of the more frequently seen images throughout all Buddhist art. It is done by holding the left palm facing upward in your lap with your right hand touching the earth. It represents a request for enlightenment.

The bodhyangi mudra is also known as *the mudra of the six elements* as well as *the fist of wisdom.* To make this gesture you grasp the index finger of your left hand with the index finger of your right hand. It is most frequently seen on statues featuring the Vairocana Buddha.

The dharmachakra mudra is also known as *the turning of the wheel mudra* and represents being completely in the moment. It is done by placing both of your hands together in front of the chest with the right palm facing forward and the left palm facing upward.

The dhyana mudra is known as *the meditation mudra* which means it is a great mudra to practice while adjusting to Kundalini meditation. To perform it, you place both of your hands in your lap with your left hand on top of your right with your fingers fully extended. Each of your four pairs of fingers should be resting on one another with your thumbs facing upwards towards one another at a diagonal angle. When done correctly your fingers and hands will form the shape of a triangle which symbolizes the spiritual fire also known as the three jewels.

INTRODUCTION TO CHAKRAS

Another important aspect of preparation for your Kundalini meditation experience is understanding the chakras.

In Sanskrit, the word chakra literally means *"wheel of light"* and that is how chakras should be looked at – as a gift, especially to those that can see them. When someone can see them, they appear as spinning colored light wheels. Each chakra appears as a different color on the rainbow spectrum.

Each chakra is aligned along the spinal column and they form the backbone that connects the body, mind, and spirit. This network includes several smaller energy centers throughout the body and typically corresponds with acupuncture points.

Foundation Chakra

Located at the bottom of your spine, you will find the foundational chakra, known as *muladhara*. It is what makes you feel like you have a body, a separate person, and an agreement and connection that your spirit is within an existence. This where the life force is rooted and active.

Sexual Center

Swadhisthana, is the second chakra. It is connected to the sexual organs, the need to procreate, or desire for pleasure. This is an active chakra, but it is typically out of balance. This can cause a sex obsession, or the polar opposite; condemnation, fear, or frigidity of the body. This is thought to be where desire is stored. This is also where the dark energies in the subconscious are held.

Power Seat

Manipura is the third chakra and is slightly below your bellybutton. This is where your personal identity lives. This is the power center and is what controls accumulation and survival. The energy quality impacts physical and psychological health, energy that moves through your organs, and your digestion.

Heart Awakening

Anahata is the fourth chakra. It is located at the center of the chest within the spine and parallel to your heart. If you lived in a world where you didn't have to experience any grief, loss, or disappointment, then, chances are, your heart chakra would stay open and loving, but when you experience pain or contraction, it creates defensiveness, protectiveness, and armor. The traits associated with the heart chakra are empathy, compassion, appreciation of people and nature, love of life, and creativity.

Opposites Awakened

Vishuddhi is the fifth chakra. This one is located behind the throat in the cervical plexus, and it affects the hearing, ears, and throat. The meaning of Shuddhi is to purify, but the work done here is more than clearing because when you transform this chakra it brings you to terms with your opposites and will give you the ability to accept and understand the light and dark of life.

Third Eye

The next chakra is the third eye chakra, also known as *Ajna*. The definition of *Ajna* is to follow or know. This chakra is slightly above and between the eyebrows. This is known as the command center of your whole subtle body system. The pineal gland is associated with this chakra, which has a tendency to shut down once you reach age 9 or 10.

Thousand Petal Lotus

The last chakra is *Sahasrara*. It is compared to a *thousand petal lotus,* and it is found at the top of your head or slightly above it. This depends on which tradition you choose to follow. Tantra views this chakra as a symbol of unlimited possibilities and having a complete realization of the truth.

CHAPTER 3

THE PRACTICAL GUIDE TO KUNDALINI MEDITATIONS

Before we get started with our guided meditation, I'd like to provide you with a set of important practical tips on preparing yourself for Kundalini.

Don't rush

There is a right way to get experience a Kundalini awakening and a wrong way to be able to get to that point. The wrong way would be *rushing things*. You need to make sure that you are following at your own individual pace and that you are always working toward getting it done the right way. There are many different options that come along with Kundalini and doing the right thing for your own body, mind and spirit experience. For some people, the steps will only take a few months or years. Others, though, may be working to achieve Kundalini for their entire lives and never get to that point.

Use help from outside

Remember that having someone help you, as a guru, is not an indicator of what you are able to do on your own and is just a sign of *acceptance*. It is not a weak thing for you to ask a guru for help and you should make sure that you know that before you start your path to Kundalini awakening. There are so many things that come along with it, and it is important that you take each of the steps seriously. If you find that you are having trouble, feel that the progress is very slow a guru will be able to project Kundalini toward you, and you will be able to benefit from that.

Practice regularly

If you get to experience a Kundalini awakening and it is active in your own mind, body, and spirit, you should continuously try to get to that place. Every time that you practice yoga, you need to make sure that you are working toward Kundalini. It is not a bad idea to try to get there with each asana so that you will be able to get the most out of the practice. It is a wise idea to try for Kundalini each time that you begin a yogic practice and each time that you work toward making things the right way.

MASTERING THE ESSENTIAL KUNDALINI MEDITATION TECHNIQUE

Begin your meditations by sitting comfortably. Start taking nice deep breaths. Many Kundalini gurus will have you say the mantra *"Ong Na Mo Guru Dev Na Mo"* to get you ready for your meditation. To do this, take one deep breath in, and on the exhale, say the mantra in one smooth line.

To hear how to say the mantra, you can listen to this <u>audio clip</u> from the Kundalini Yoga site (<u>www.Kundaliniyoga.org/lesson 3</u>). Do this cycle three times before beginning your meditation.

Kundalini meditations are supposed to be done within certain times. Meditations can be done in increments of three, eleven, twenty-two, thirty-one, sixty-two, and two and a half hours. Various parts of the body and mind activate and change during each time period. The longer the meditation, the better the effect it will have on your body and mind. Three minutes begins to affect your circulation, after thirty-one minutes your cells begin to change, and after two and a half hours your entire mind changes.

After forty days, you are beginning the habit. After ninety days, you are confirming the habit, getting it set into your routine and making it a part of your life. After one hundred and twenty days, you become the habit, making it a part of you. After one thousand days, you will have mastered the habit, having it permanently instilled into your life and being.

Human beings are creatures of habit. Habits rule our lives. Changing one single habit for the better can change your entire life. Take the time for these meditations daily and this small habit can change your life for the better.

Step One

When it comes to practicing a technique to prepare yourself for a Kundalini awakening, the first thing you are going to want to do is to focus on your breathing, starting with the inhale as the breath flows through your body, all the way from the base of your spine to the top of your head. As the breath moves up your body, you are going to want to focus on the path it is taking and the energy that can follow that same path.

During this period, you are going to want to remain focused on your breathing without forcing the process to occur. Kundalini meditation is never about forcing anything; it is about opening yourself up to the possibility of the Kundalini awakening. With a little practice, you will be able to do this as a way of priming the energy to move through your body. Once you can feel the energy begin to rise at the base of your spine, you will know that you are ready for the second step in the process.

Step Two

Once you have gotten into the habit of inhaling properly, you will want to expand this process until you can exhale properly as well. To do so, as you exhale you are going to want to make a conscious effort to push the air through the third eye, down your throat, past the heart chakra and then release when you are near the center of your chest. This should ensure that the energy continues to build within your body instead of allowing it to continuously rise and fall.

During a guided Kundalini awakening, it is common for a Kundalini master to bestow *shaktipat*, the actual awakening, upon their students either by chanting with them, focusing energy on them or even touching them. To recreate this process at home, the first thing you will need to do is to go through the previous parts of the exercise before doing whatever you need to do in order to focus in on an audio recording of a speaker you enjoy who is extremely enlightened.

From there, you will want to try and focus will all of your mental might on the energy that they are projecting while they speak. The goal should be to harness their secondary energy in such a way that it helps to bring about your own Kundalini awakening. Once you have spent some time really focusing on the person whose energy you are using you will want to go ahead and make them a part of your daily process and when you inhale and exhale their name should be on your lips as well.

It is important to always keep in mind that the Kundalini is within you at all times and your practices are only serving to bring it out within yourself. This is why it is not something to be nervous about, you are not inviting something into yourself, you are awakening a dormant part of yourself that will change your life for the better. For the best results, you will want to wholeheartedly embrace any and all feelings that come over you.

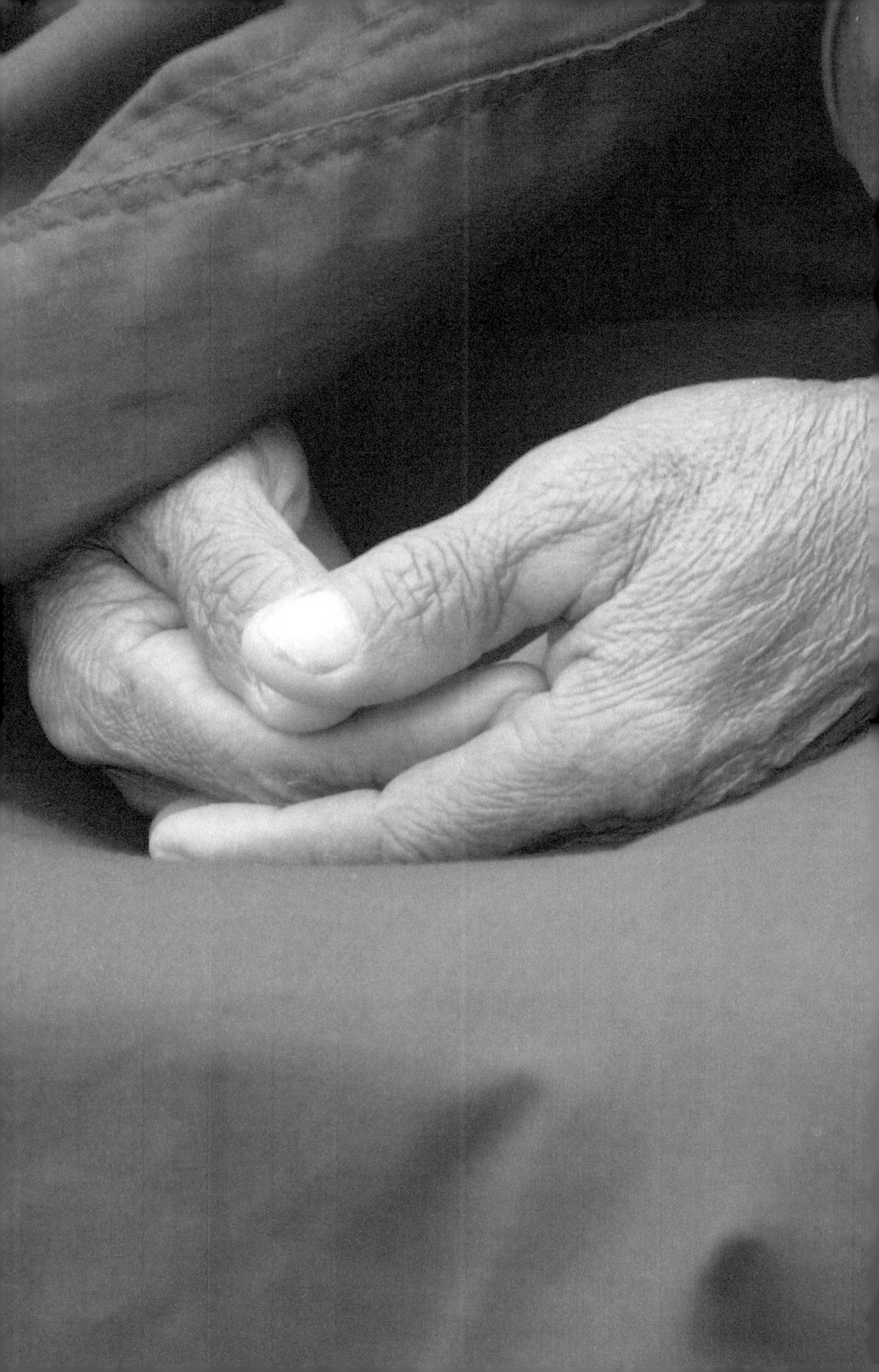

CHAPTER 4

❈

PREPARATION AND LOGISTICS

Now, the time has come to prepare yourself for the guided meditations. First of all, you will need to make yourself physically comfortable in a safe space in which you can unwind and open yourself to cosmic energies.

Ready your environment. Declutter your surroundings. Create a space that will not distract you from navigating your own spiritual journey. Perhaps light a scented candle or a stick of incense. A soothing aroma may help guide your senses to a more pleasurable frame of mind. A sweet wave of lavender or vanilla may provide you with a calmness otherwise unfounded in your chosen space of meditation. The earthy tones of sandalwood or lemongrass may help lull you into a trance, a state of mind susceptible to spiritual guidance. You may prefer nectarous scents like a mandarin orange or red apple. Let the candle's flame flicker. Let the incense stick pour its smoke.

Perhaps, brew yourself a cup of herbal tea. Establish a connection with nature by ingesting a steeped herb, flower, or root. Allow the sweet, earthy liquid to clear your nasal passages. Unencumbered breathing is integral to meditation. A steaming cup of tea will warm your insides and loosen your muscles by relieving them of unwanted stress. It will help your body sink into your meditation. Let the tea replenish your body with essential antioxidants and vitamins. Tune your body with this natural remedy.

Are you wearing comfortable clothing? It is crucial that what you are wearing does not inhibit your ability to breathe. Loose fitting clothing or breathable fabrics are recommended. Is the temperature of your space to your liking? Will a lack or excess of warmth or cold break your concentration? Adjust your setting. Create a space that's right for you.

Choose a spot to sit or lie down. Do not engage in meditation while engaged in other activities like walking or driving. Your body must be stationary, you must be open and ready to receive spiritual guidance. Allow yourself to concentrate on the journey ahead.

Perhaps you have a favorite chair in which to sit on. A bed, a couch, or a cushioned mat on the floor are also acceptable places to situate yourself for a session of meditation. Fluff your pillows or cushions. Ready your favorite fuzzy blanket. Maybe employ a face mask to black out your surroundings. Allow your body to sink into whatever space you choose.

Distance yourself from polluting noise. It is unideal to allow in loud engines on the road, trains chugging past, loud voices outside your window, rattling footsteps, dogs barking, cats hissing, dump trucks clunking along, or the ringing of a phone. Silence your phone and shut down your computer. Separate yourself from the noise. Use headphones or a loud enough speaker set to listen to the meditations. Submerge yourself in the journey, and eliminate any possible distractions. All five senses must be wholly committed to the journey in order to achieve ultimate relaxation.

CHAPTER 5

GUIDED KUNDALINI MEDITATIONS

In this chapter I would like to share with you my guided meditations which aim to balance your inner energy. The ultimate goal is to help you feel grounded and content. First, I will I guide you into a **deep state of relaxation**. Then we will continue with **Kundalini meditations**.

THE PATH TO RELAXATION

Please, proceed to **page 37** to follow the
included guided meditation.

First Kundalini Meditation

Inhale deeply through your nose.

Concentrate on filling your abdomen.

Exhale deeply from your mouth.

Feel as life flows through you.

From the blackness behind your closed lids
emerges a ball of light. This ball of light is
suspended below your belly, it is in your lap.
This radiating force represents the potential glow
of your root chakra.

Feel its red warmth.

It holds a precious power, a blessed virtue.

Do you feel your own Muladhara?

How far does its energy extend within you?

What is keeping it from flourishing?

True peace and unadulterated bliss do not come from material gain. Your possessions are not your purpose.
There is more to the universe than money and power.
Take this time to connect with the waves around you.

Second Kundalini Meditation

The ball of light moves from you.

It gently beckons you to follow.

From the blackness behind your closed lids, you

follow the benign orb on the path it wanders.

In your heart, you know the path is paved with

revelation.

You are drawn by an electrifying sensation to

follow the ball of light.

You feel this current coursing through your veins.

The orb guides you to a curtain in the blackness.

You slip your hand through the small opening in

which it went.

The curtain is satin, the material feels cool against
your radiating skin.
You step through to find a grassy cove at the
bottom of a green valley.
Trees dance in the wind.
You hear water dancing in a river close by.
The ball of light is waiting for you in a clearing of
soft grass.
The sun shines on the orb, the two are one and the
same.

THIRD KUNDALINI MEDITATION

The grass folds beneath your feet.

The earth supports your journey.

As you walk closer to the ball of light, your

Muladhara stirs with vivacity.

You feel your primal energy circulating more

freely with every step you take.

You feel the warmth it holds emanating from the

base of your spine.

Concentrate on that energy.

Breathe in through your nose.

Exhale through your mouth.

The sun shining down can be felt in every nerve of

your body.

Your body gratefully accepts the rays.
You hear bushes rustling to your left.
A lynx emerges.
You are secure.
The animal is not here to stop your journey.
The animal respects your presence in this valley of
enlightenment. You nod to the beautiful creature
and continue towards the light.

The orb moves onward.
It does not rush.
You do not rush after it.
Your Muladhara produces a faint current.
The pleasant charge runs through your legs and
carries you forward.

Fourth Kundalini Meditation

The ball of light once again stops.

It waits for you now by a softly roaring fire.

The sticks and wood crackle, the smell makes you

feel safe.

You walk closer to see a bowl of crystal-clear

water.

It glistens in the light.

You sit cross-legged by the gentle fire and pick up

the bowl.

You bring it to your lips and take a sip.

The cool water runs down your throat and into

your belly.

The water soothes and heals your insides.

The water purifies your voice, it washes out any
dishonesty spoken in the near past.
You take a bigger gulp.
Your thirst is now quenched.

You set the bowl down.
The light gently bobs from across the fire.
The orange flames ripple.
You admire the conviction of the fire's dance.
You inhale the clean air.
The sky is happy to provide you with this breath of
life.
You are thankful for the air that fills you.

Fifth Kundalini Meditation

The glowing orb of light gradually makes its way
through a thicket of trees.

You stand up and follow.

You extend your hands to feel the coarse surface of
the greenery surrounding you.

The forest is thriving with life.

The forest welcomes you as a valued member of its
peaceful community.

The orb continues weaving through the sturdy
trunks of trees.

Leaves and sticks crunch beneath your feet.

The shade from the canopy puts you in a deeper
state of ease.

The light stops in a large patch of a sunbeam.

You follow its unspoken guidance and sit in that
beam.

You feel the earth under your palms.

The soil is rich and cool, it is giving and caring.

You are temperate at this time.

You are undisturbed in this place.

Sixth Kundalini Meditation

You are seated in the soil.

Your Muladhara is uncoiling enough to reveal a seedling in its place.

It is waiting to bud.

You are a receptacle of a unique life.

This seedling slowly grows its roots within you.

It slowly grows its roots into the soil beneath you.

You are deeply connected to the earth and all its inhabitants.

You are a piece of an incredible whole.

The seed is unconcerned with matters of material, unconcerned with shallow subjects.

You are the holder of this pure form of life energy.

You feel its power traveling up your spine.

It starts at the base.

It moves up slowly.

It vibrates your core.

The water you consumed earlier is nurturing the
seed.

It is readying itself to sprout.

You, in turn, are readying yourself to be a healthy
home for this power to grow.

Seventh Kundalini Meditation

The orb of light grows closer to you.

You feel the seed at the base of your spine break

out of its shell.

The sensation is warm, it radiates power.

It harnesses the truth.

You are a vessel of power and truth.

Live honestly.

Live with a purpose for this world.

The light is inches from you.

You tingle with zeal for the light's energy.

It moves closer.

You breathe in deeply.

The light moves inside you to the base of your
spine.
You exhale deeply.
The seed flourishes into a magnificent spectacle
within you.
You are the shelter, the keeper, and the nurturer of
its power.
You must treat this gift with respect.
Respect for yourself, respect for all life around you.
You have a home anywhere on this earth.

THE RETURN

Now that you have absorbed and connected fully
with the light, you must cross through the curtain
once more.

You must come back from this journey.

Take a moment to access how you feel.

Take a deep breath in.

Release.

Are you satisfied with the state of your mind and
body?

Are you in touch with your primal energy?

I hope you are feeling confident in your ability to
survive in the life you have and will create for
yourself.

You must now get up from the patch of sun in
which you sit.

Take this moment to reflect on the aspects of your
life that warm you every day.

A friend?

A lover?

An animal companion?

Your own self-love?

Thank the forest around you, say goodbye to its
protective canopy.

As you walk, appreciate the time this environment
took to grow on its own.

Nature has been self-sustaining since the dawn of
time.

Respect it and imitate its growth.

You re-emerge from the forest and pass the
dwindling fire.

Reflect on the aspects of your life that kindle a
flame within you.

What are your passions?

Do you devote enough time and energy to them?

You nod at the bowl of water.

Reflect on what hydrates you.

What refreshes your mind, body, and spirit?

You continue on and re-encounter the lynx you met earlier.

The lack of confrontation with the small beast should remind you to confront your fears.

Do not assume the worst just because you can.

Kindness takes many forms.

Pet the lynx.

Its fur is soft to your touch.

It mutters a purr and retreats into the forest.

You see your exit just ahead.

Before leaving, take a moment for yourself.

Focus on the energy at the base of your spine, focus on your awakened kundalini.

Feel the heat of its power run through you.

Namaste.

CONCLUSION

Thanks for making it through to the end of *Spiritual Energy Healing: Kundalini*. I sincerely hope that reading this book was useful for you and I successfully guided you through refreshingly new or comfortably familiar ways to achieve inner peace. It's important to consistently acknowledge the energies working around you, how the energies affect you, and how you affect those energies. Be sure to constantly remind yourself that you are merely a small piece of a greater whole. Yet, just as the universe is infinitely expanding, so are you.

The next step is to make a ritual of your preferred meditation. Practicing every day helps guarantee the results you want to experience from meditation. Daily discipline will improve your concentration and ground your thoughts during your sacred times of personal rumination. Embed positivity within you. Don't sweat the small aspects of life.

You can also explore more resources that help you unlock deeper levels of harmony. To advance your spiritual journey, discover more about the practices and teachings of Hinduism, Buddhism, and holistic Japanese techniques. Eastern cultures have an array of deeply spiritual history packed full of wisdom. Perhaps pay a visit to a Reiki healer near you. You may also enjoy yoga as a more physically involved form of meditation that utilizes similar meditative techniques found in my book.

With much love,
Anne Brennan

SPIRITUAL ENERGY HEALING

The ultimate introduction and guided Mindfulness meditation for relaxation, better sleep, stress and anxiety relief

ANNE BRENNAN

CHAPTER 1

INTRODUCTION TO MINDFULNESS

While it has been a part of the Buddhist faith for more than two thousand years, mindfulness meditation has become exceedingly popular in the Western world over the past several decades thanks to its proven ability to improve mental health including the treatment of stress, anxiety and even drug addiction.

The idea of practicing mindfulness first caught on in the Western world in the early part of the 1970s. Professor *Jon Kabat-Zinn* is credited with creating a mindfulness based method of stress reduction which paired mindfulness with yoga to great result.

While Zinn didn't do anything particularly new, the fact that his techniques led to measurable improvements for a wide variety of ailments both mental and physical in turn led to additional studies on the topic. These studies have shown time and again how effective practicing mindfulness can be which in turn has led to a steady increase in the practice to the point where it can now be found being regularly practiced in schools, veteran treatment facilities, hospitals, even prisons.

What' s more, additional studies show that that taking 15 minutes out of your day to practice mindfulness meditation has a host of additional benefits as well. For starters, it is known to show dramatic increases when it comes to projecting a strong sense of self while at the same time noticeably reducing stress. This is thanks to the positive effects that mindfulness meditation has on attention span, emotional regulation and body awareness. What's even more impressive, neuroimaging has shown that mindfulness meditation actually allows those who practice it to process information more quickly than those who do not.

OTHER REASONS TO PRACTICE MINDFULNESS MEDITATION

- Mindfulness meditation naturally leads to a deeper understanding of the self and allows many people to take stock of their strengths and weaknesses, leading to personal growth.

- Studies show that those who practice mindfulness regularly have a stronger memory, leading to an easier retention of facts in both the long and the short term.

- In addition to the specifics, mindfulness meditation improves overall physical wellbeing with those who practice regularly reporting fewer instances of illness and a more rapid recovery when they do fall ill.

- Mindfulness meditation can help improve emotional control while at the same time increasing one's threshold for pain.

- As surprising as it might seem, making a habit of being mindful can actually make even the most middling music seem more engaging. This deeper level of engagement leads to a general increase in enjoyment, regardless of the type of music or any previous musical preferences.

- With a regular dose of mindfulness meditation, many people experience a dramatic increase in their ability to empathize with others no matter what the situation. Furthermore, it allows practitioners to listen to other viewpoints more actively, more compassionately and results in their ability to withhold judgement on thoughts and ideas that differ from their own.

Since its inception, mindfulness meditation been proven via scientific study to improve the physical wellbeing of those that practice it on a regular basis. At its heart, mindfulness meditation is all about *focusing your mind to ensure that you are as fully aware of each moment as fully as possible*. This, in turn, allows you to exist more completely in any given moment by expanding your consciousness to the fullest.

While it might sound like a tall order at first, the truth of the matter is that being mindful is a skill which means it can be improved by regular practice in much the same way as any other skill. Luckily, practicing mindfulness meditation is as easy as finding a few moments to focus solely on the present and the information that your senses are providing you at the moment. In fact, if you can find just fifteen minutes a day to practice, you will soon find that your overall stress is likely to decrease and your sense of self is likely to be at an all-time high. This isn't just an ephemeral feeling either, neuroimaging performed on those who practice mindfulness meditation on a regular basis, shows that their minds actually process information more effectively. They are able to more easily regulate their emotions and their attention spans than those who do not make the practice a part of their daily routine.

Furthermore, the sooner you begin practicing mindfulness meditation, the greater the chance that doing so will ensure your brain retains more volume as you age, dramatically improving overall brain health as a result. This increased vitality also reaches the hippocampus (*a part of the limbic system which amongst other things is responsible for memory*) which, in turn, makes it easier to learn and retain new information with minimal effort. At the same time, the amygdala (*another part of the limbic system, which amongst other things is responsible for processing emotions*) becomes less active which means that the amount of fear, stress, and anxiety that you experience will be decreased as well.

While mindfulness can be practiced almost anywhere at nearly any time, the concept began as a structured meditation technique practiced by Buddhists known as *vipassana*. Roughly translated this means to *live in the moment while understanding that sometimes you must be aware of the future as well*. The general idea is that achieving *vipassana* will allow you to come to understand the universe as a whole and comes through the knowing of a few key principals.

Generally known as the three marks of existence, non-self, dissatisfaction, and impermanence are thought of as the three factors which unite all living things. The idea behind non-self is that you must know where the world ends and you begin and that by focusing on this definition you may better understand both sides of it. The idea of dissatisfaction comes from the fact that striving to find satisfaction in temporary things is inherently a flawed notion. This is because of the fact that all living things are impermanent and you must come to terms with that fact if you wish to find peace.

CHAPTER 2

THE PRACTICAL GUIDE TO MINDFULNESS MEDITATIONS

HOW TO PRACTICE MINDFULNESS MEDITATIONS

Unlike other types of meditation, being mindful doesn't require a large time commitment or a space that is quite and calm for a specific period of time. While these things will certainly help you get into the required mindset at first, eventually you will find that you can get your mindfulness on while at the gym, doing chores or even commuting to and from work. Regardless of where you do it, the basics of mindfulness mediation are always the same.

STICK WITH A SPECIFIC TIME

As with any new habit, it is crucial that you create a routine around your mindfulness meditation practices for the best results. Generally speaking, you can expect it to take about 30 days for a new habit to really stick which means that you will need to commit to going hard for just four weeks before you can expect to start seeing the best results.

Unfortunately, due to its few requirements and low impact nature, it is often quite easy to push off your set mindfulness meditation time for a later than never comes, especially if they are already very busy as it stands. If you find yourself always coming up with an excuse to get out of meditating at the moment, you may find the following piece of advice particularly useful. "Practice mindfulness meditation for fifteen minutes every day unless, of course, you are extremely busy in which case you should practice for thirty minutes instead." Don't let the outside world intrude on your potential for inner peace, find a time each day that works for you and stick with it no matter what; in a month's time, you will be glad you did.

In order to reach a state of mindfulness, you are going to want to find someplace comfortable, and quiet to sit, though not so quiet and comfortable that you are tempted to fall asleep. Then, all you need to do is breathe deeply, in and out.

Start by doing your best to calm your mind by taking a few deep breaths and then announce your intentions aloud to make them more tangible. From there, take several more, deep breaths and focus on the sensations that your senses are providing you as you do so. Consider how your lungs feel as they expand and the smells this action brings to your attention. If you are sitting, consider the feel of the chair on your skin, the temperature of the room and the movement of any wind across your skin. Let the sensations flow from one to another, working their way down your body completely.

Continue breathing deeply but keep your eyes and ears alert and providing you with more information than you previously thought possible. Focus on this information to the exclusion of everything else. You will likely find it difficult to shut out the constant flow of information that is running through your mind relating to things you need to do, regrets over past actions and plans that must be made, but this is completely normal. If you find your focus drifting away from the moment, take note of the mistake and move on. There is nothing to be gained from beating yourself up over it and you will only take yourself out of the moment even more.

Once you have reached a relaxed state, to remove the excess thoughts that are likely running through your head, all you need to do is picture them as a stream of bubbles that are rushing by in front of your eyes. Simply take a step back and let the thoughts flow past you without interacting with them. If one of them catches your attention and draws you into more complex thought, simply disengage and let it go. Don't focus on the fact that you were thinking about it, because that will just draw you out of the moment, simply remain in that state for as long as possible. Eventually, this will help with negative thoughts you experience in the real world as well.

In fact, with enough time and practice, you will likely find that you are able to maintain a mild meditative state even when you are otherwise focused on the world around you. This is known as a state of mindfulness and it should be the end goal of everyone who is new to the meditative practice. Being mindful means always being connected to a calming and soothing mental state as well as one that is full of joy and peace which benefits not just yourself but everyone around you.

Mindfulness is not necessarily quieting the mind or finding an eternal state of calmness. The goal here is simple. You want to pay attention to the moment you are in without judging it. When you judge a thought or something you may have done in the past, you likely, tend to dwell on it. That isn't living in the moment and is not conducive to mindful meditation. While this is easier said than done, it is a crucial step to mindful meditation. With practice, it will be easy to achieve. Be mindful of the moment, of your senses and your surroundings.

Take notice of the times you are passing judgment while practicing mindfulness. Make note of them and move on. It is easy for your mind to get lost in thought. Mindfulness meditation is the art of bringing yourself back to the moment, over and over, as many times as it takes. Don't get discouraged. In the beginning, you will find your mind wanders a lot. Reel it back in and keep moving forward. Even if your mind does happen to wander, and it will, don't be hard on yourself. It happens. Acknowledge whatever thoughts pop up, put them to the side and get back on track.

When you first start practicing mindfulness meditation it is very important that you do so under the understanding that you aren't going to see any results from your hard work at first and rather need to commit to the process fully before you can start receiving any rewards. Specifically, you will need to keep in mind that it is natural for your mind to wander freely for a time before you are able to guide it to where it needs to be. To better understand the mindset that you should be striving for, you might find it useful to consider the moment of complete blankness the mind experiences once it has heard a question but before it can generate an answer.

OTHER WAYS OF BEING MINDFUL

SHOWERING

While many people operate on autopilot while in the shower, you can use this opportunity to give yourself a boost of mindfulness instead. This is because the senses are already in overdrive in the shower which means it is easier to get into the moment than it may be in other situations.

EXERCISE

While it might seem surprising, the mental state that the body finds itself in while exercising is actually quite close to a state of mindfulness, to begin with, which means it doesn't take much to push it over the edge. To get in the zone, consider the way your body feels as each muscle exerts itself as you push it to the limit.

CHORES

The repetitive nature of most chores makes them a perfect outlet for a bit of mindfulness. To make the most of these tasks, all you need to do is clear your mind beforehand and then focus on all the sensations working through the task provides you. When you are finished, consider how much better off you are now that the chore is completed and reflect on your ability to positively affect your environment.

SOCIAL MEDIA

While making a more concentrated attempt to single-task will ultimately help you practice mindfulness more easily. Until you decide to do away with social media distractions completely, consider using them in a mindful manner instead. The next time you find yourself looking through old photographs, use that time to really remember the moment that each photograph was taken. Strain your memory and try and recall everything you can about the situation. What were the smells, the sounds, the sights? How did you feel at the moment? Really work to try and get back to that place to the extent that you block out external stimuli.

THE END RESULT

While there are plenty of proven positive side effects of practicing mindfulness, most of them are difficult to track on your own without specialized equipment as they occur at a physical level you can't see or occur on a mental level which is difficult to observe without bias. Instead, you will likely know that you are on the right track when you start to see changes to the mental conditioning you have been living with your entire life.

Modern society often instills in individuals a desire to hide their flaws and to treat any uncomfortable feelings or thoughts they have in much the same way. Over time, this leads to a desire to revise the truth and rewrite history, so it shows things in a more positive light overall. Despite not being an especially healthy way to deal with existing issues, this common habit actually stems from the well-known flight or fight reflex that helped humanity's ancestors survive against threats regardless if they were real or imagined.

While this impulse helped your ancient ancestors survive, and even thrive, amongst the harsh conditions they lived with day to day, these days, if left unchecked, it can instead easily lead to a scenario where it undermines the qualities and traits that make you unique. This, in turn, leads us to one of the greatest benefits of mindfulness. It provides those who practice it with a greater understanding of themselves which is the first step to a greater acceptance of their strengths and weaknesses and the ways the two can be used together for the best results.

Regularly practicing mindfulness, and sticking with it in the long-term, can replace this negative mindset with one that is much more positive which is referred to as radical acceptance. Simply put, radical acceptance allows you to more easily get in touch with the things you are experiencing or feeling in the moment, without having to worry about societal filters getting in the way.

CHAPTER 3

THE PATH TO MINDFULNESS

PREPARATION AND LOGISTICS

Now, the time has come to prepare yourself for the guided meditations. First of all, you will need to make yourself physically comfortable in a safe space in which you can unwind and open yourself to cosmic energies.

Ready your environment. Declutter your surroundings. Create a space that will not distract you from navigating your own spiritual journey. Perhaps light a scented candle or a stick of incense. A soothing aroma may help guide your senses to a more pleasurable frame of mind. A sweet wave of lavender or vanilla may provide you with a calmness otherwise unfounded in your chosen space of meditation. The earthy tones of sandalwood or lemongrass may help lull you into a trance, a state of mind susceptible to spiritual guidance. You may prefer nectarous scents like a mandarin orange or red apple. Let the candle's flame flicker. Let the incense stick pour its smoke.

Perhaps, brew yourself a cup of herbal tea. Establish a connection with nature by ingesting a steeped herb, flower, or root. Allow the sweet, earthy liquid to clear your nasal passages. Unencumbered breathing is integral to meditation. A steaming cup of tea will warm your insides and loosen your muscles by relieving them of unwanted stress. It will help your body sink into your meditation. Let the tea replenish your body with essential antioxidants and vitamins. Tune your body with this natural remedy.

Are you wearing comfortable clothing? It is crucial that what you are wearing does not inhibit your ability to breathe. Loose fitting clothing or breathable fabrics are recommended. Is the temperature of your space to your liking? Will a lack or excess of warmth or cold break your concentration? Adjust your setting. Create a space that's right for you.

Choose a spot to sit or lie down. Do not engage in meditation while engaged in other activities like walking or driving. Your body must be stationary, you must be open and ready to receive spiritual guidance. Allow yourself to concentrate on the journey ahead.

Perhaps you have a favorite chair in which to sit on. A bed, a couch, or a cushioned mat on the floor are also acceptable places to situate yourself for a session of meditation. Fluff your pillows or cushions. Ready your favorite fuzzy blanket. Maybe employ a face mask to black out your surroundings. Allow your body to sink into whatever space you choose.

Distance yourself from polluting noise. It is unideal to allow in loud engines on the road, trains chugging past, loud voices outside your window, rattling footsteps, dogs barking, cats hissing, dump trucks clunking along, or the ringing of a phone. Silence your phone and shut down your computer. Separate yourself from the noise. Use headphones or a loud enough speaker set to listen to the meditations. Submerge yourself in the journey, and eliminate any possible distractions. All five senses must be wholly committed to the journey in order to achieve ultimate relaxation.

In this and the next chapters I would like to share with you my guided meditations which aim to balance your inner energy. The ultimate goal is to help you feel grounded and content. First, I will I guide you into a *deep state of relaxation*. Then we will continue with *Mindfulness meditations*.

THE PATH TO RELAXATION

Please, proceed to **page 37** to follow the included guided meditation.

CHAPTER 4

GUIDED MINDFULNESS MEDITATIONS

THE POINT OF ENTRY – STAGE 1

We will begin these mindful meditations by breathing using a *"sohum"* mantra. Direct your focus to the air filling and leaving your lungs. Pay attention to the stream of breath as it enters through your mouth, as it travels down your windpipe, as your diaphragm rises, as your lungs swell.

Start by exhaling through your nose. Exhale the sound *"hum"* and focus on your diaphragm concaving as you release. Once all air has been released from your body, take a deep breath in through y our mouth and drag out the word *"so."*

Good.

Repeat the process. Exhale with a purposeful *"hum"*, inhale with a concentrated *"so."* You are slipping into a state of relaxation worthy of the mindfulness you are about to exercise.

THE POINT OF ENTRY – STAGE 2

The following meditations require you to form a new sphere of imagination. Place yourself in a *fruit orchard* of your choosing. You are about to embark on a stroll down rows of your favorite fruit hanging from the branches and vines.

The orchard fills your nose with balm, sweet scents that make your tongue tingle with desire.

You have an empty wicker basket under your arm.

Birds are singing within the rows of greenery.

The sun shines down purifying rays of gold.

You are ready to fill your basket with the fresh harvest from this land.

This place is a piece of your personal Eden.

First Mindfulness Meditation

You are surveying the orchard.

Vibrant fruits hang from branches, dangle from vines.

These fruits are the things you cherish the most.

You've grown this crop with time, with love, with care, and attention.

You nurtured these entities of happiness and joy.

They are ripe for your hands to pluck.

With basket in the arm, you make your way down one of the many aisles of springing life.

Bountiful trees and bushes sway in the gentle breeze.

They wave at you.

They greet their caretaker with a dance.

You have watered and fed them.

You've nurtured each relationship, your heart

swells with reciprocated love.

Second Mindfulness Meditation

While walking through the orchard, your eyes

catch a fruit.

It shines in the ascending sun rays.

You make your way over to the fruit.

You gingerly take the fruit, it eagerly snaps off

its branch for you.

It is smooth in your palm.

Its new home is in your wicker basket.

The basket's weight adjusts to the new fruit.

You welcome the new responsibility of the lone

produce.

It relies on your consideration of its life to make

it to its next home.

You feel great respect for the life growing
around you.

You slowly take new steps.
The breeze sends honeyed scents into your nose.
You breathe it in with deep pleasure.

THIRD MINDFULNESS MEDITATION

The orchard's soil is soft beneath your bare feet.

You continue down the aisle, more produce awaits.

Your basket beings to fill with carefully chosen
fruit.

Your arms are thankful for the weight they carry.

It is not a burden.

The sweat that glistens on your forehead baptizes
you.

You are an essential element in this universe.

The cycle of life prevails despite hardships.

You have the power to cause change, to make a
difference.

Your arms throbbing with helpful purpose.

You stop walking.

You exhale through your nose.

You inhale through your parted mouth.

You look down at the earth's ground.

It welcomes you to sit, to relieve the pressure of

standing.

You accept the earth's invitation.

Fourth Mindfulness Meditation

You place your basket on the ground beside you.

You let your bottom mold to the soil.

You exhale through your nose.

You inhale through a parted mouth.

You pick a soft fruit from the peak of your basket's

mound.

It is smooth in your palm.

You bring it up to your mouth and take a bite.

You pierce the skin with your teeth.

On the inside, the fruit is hydrating.

You chew. You savor. You swallow.

The food runs down through your body.

Your body thanks you.

You are filled with its vitamins and antioxidants.

The fruit is giving back to you what you gave to it.

You discard the fruit's remains on the ground.

You give back to the earth what it gave to you.

Exhale through your nose.

Inhale through a parted mouth.

FIFTH MINDFULNESS MEDITATION

You smell a storm approaching.

Overhead, you see a gray cloud rolling towards you.

It gradually blocks the sun.

The smell of rain rustles through the orchard leaves.

Your hair is tousled by the wind.

The sky has been summoned to water the surrounding life.

You stand up with your full basket.

You walk toward a gazebo in the center of the orchard.

You let the first drops of rain fall on your head and
open palms.

The drops are cool.

The drops are refreshing.

Under the shelter, you find an empty canvas
perched on an easel.

Beside the canvas stands an array of paint.

There are paints of every color.

Crimson, butterscotch, scarlet, maroon, mint, olive,
sunflower, and navy.

All the colors you can imagine and more.

You set down your basket on a table beside the
canvas.

You step up to the canvas as the rain starts to fall
around you.

Sixth Mindfulness Meditation

What will you paint?

Envision your masterpiece.

You still taste the sweet fruit on your tongue.

You still smell the earth's dirt on your fingertips.

The paint is natural and pure, the paint is odorless.

You pick up a paintbrush.

Your mind buzzes with creativity.

You know in your heart that every stroke has a
purpose, every stroke is beautiful.

You can make no mistake on this blank canvas.

You dip the bristles of the brush into a can of paint.

The paint is smooth, it is creamy, and it is ready to
help bring your vision to fruition.

Seventh Mindfulness Meditation

You exhale through your nose.

You inhale through a parted mouth.

You take the tip of the paintbrush out of the can.

The color looks radiant on the brush.

You bring it to the canvas and make a mighty

sweep over its surface.

The color comes to life.

You rinse the brush in a cup of water beside the

easel.

You carefully dip the paintbrush in a new shade of

paint.

You aim to channel positivity.

You make another stroke.

The brush slides over the canvas.

Repeat this process until your masterpiece has formed itself inside your mind.

The Return

Look at your completed painting.

Allow yourself to feel pride in your work.

You created beauty with your hands.

It may be a scene of nature: a desert, a glacier, a

river, or a mountain.

Maybe it is a person you love and cherish.

Perhaps it is a concept or an object.

Whatever it is, each stroke was purposeful.

Each stroke translated a powerful message.

What colors did you choose?

Did the colors choose you?

What were your intentions with the painting?

What does it represent to you?

Did you succeed in channeling positivity onto the

canvas?...

Know that your painting is a masterpiece.

Have faith in your own abilities.

Utilize your eye for detail.

Try to notice things that you don't typically look

out for in your day-to-day life.

Appreciate those small things.

There is beauty everywhere you turn.

You simply have to identify it.

Give your painting one last long look.

Breathe in.

Release your breath…

Turn away from the painting.

Look out onto the open expanse of the fruit

orchard.

Has the rain cleared up?...

Are drops still pouring from the sky?

Do not let yourself become frustrated by things

that you cannot control.

Learn to adapt, learn to thrive in whatever
situation the universe may bring to you.
There is a lesson to be learned in every hardship…

What fruit orchard did you choose to wander
through?...
Peach… apple… mango… avocado… grape…
pomegranate…
papaya… cherry…
Was the fruit that you ate ripe?...
Was it prematurely plucked?

Do you feel like you're nourishing your
relationships?
Are they nourishing you?
Do you tend to your orchard often enough?
Is the fruit growing?
Is the fruit healthy?
Reflect on the time and energy you give to those
closest to you.

Reflect on the time and energy you give to
yourself.

Namaste.

CONCLUSION

Thanks for making it through to the end of *Spiritual Energy Healing: Mindfulness*. I sincerely hope that reading this book was useful for you and I successfully guided you through refreshingly new or comfortably familiar ways to achieve inner peace. It's important to consistently acknowledge the energies working around you, how the energies affect you, and how you affect those energies. Be sure to constantly remind yourself that you are merely a small piece of a greater whole. Yet, just as the universe is infinitely expanding, so are you.

The next step is to make a ritual of your preferred meditation. Practicing every day helps guarantee the results you want to experience from meditation. Daily discipline will improve your concentration and ground your thoughts during your sacred times of personal rumination. Embed positivity within you. Don't sweat the small aspects of life.

You can also explore more resources that help you unlock deeper levels of harmony. To advance your spiritual journey, discover more about the practices and teachings of

Hinduism, Buddhism, and holistic Japanese techniques. Eastern cultures have an array of deeply spiritual history packed full of wisdom. You may also enjoy yoga as a more physically involved form of meditation that utilizes similar meditative techniques found in my book.

With much love,
Anne Brennan